What is Kumon?

Kumon is the world's largest supplemental education provider and a leader in producing outstanding results. After-school programs in math and reading at Kumon Centers around the globe have been helping children succeed for 50 years.

Kumon Workbooks represent just a fraction of our complete curriculum of preschool-to-college-level material assigned at Kumon Centers under the supervision of trained Kumon Instructors.

The Kumon Method enables each child to progress successfully by practicing material until concepts are mastered and advancing in small, manageable increments. Instructors carefully assign materials and pace advancement according to the strengths and needs of each individual student.

Students usually attend a Kumon Center twice a week and practice at home the other five days. Assignments take about twenty minutes.

Kumon helps students of all ages and abilities master the basics, improve concentration and study habits, and build confidence.

How did Kumon begin?

IT ALL BEGAN IN JAPAN 50 YEARS AGO when a parent and teacher named Toru Kumon found a way to help his son Takeshi do better in school. At the prompting of his wife, he created a series of short assignments that his son could complete successfully in less than 20 minutes a day and that would ultimately make high school math easy. Because each was just a bit more challenging than the last, Takeshi was able to master the skills and gain the confidence to keep advancing.

This unique self-learning method was so successful that Toru's son was able to do calculus by the time he was in the sixth grade. Understanding the value of good reading comprehension, Mr. Kumon then developed a reading program employing the same method. His programs are the basis and inspiration of those offered at Kumon Centers today under the expert guidance of professional Kumon Instructors.

Mr. Toru Kumon
Founder of Kumon

What can Kumon do for my child?

Kumon is geared to children of all ages and skill levels. Whether you want to give your child a leg up in his or her schooling, build a strong foundation for future studies or address a possible learning problem, Kumon provides an effective program for developing key learning skills given the strengths and needs of each individual child.

What makes Kumon so different?

Kumon uses neither a classroom model nor a tutoring approach. It's designed to facilitate self-acquisition of the skills and study habits needed to improve academic performance. This empowers children to succeed on their own, giving them a sense of accomplishment that fosters further achievement. Whether for remedial work or enrichment, a child advances according to individual ability and initiative to reach his or her full potential. Kumon is not only effective, but also surprisingly affordable.

What is the role of the Kumon Instructor?

Kumon Instructors regard themselves more as mentors or coaches than teachers in the traditional sense. Their principal role is to provide the direction, support and encouragement that will guide the student to performing at 100% of his or her potential. Along with their rigorous training in the Kumon Method, all Kumon Instructors share a passion for education and an earnest desire to help children succeed.

KUMON FOSTERS:

- A mastery of the basics of reading and math
- Improved concentration and study habits
- Increased self-discipline and self-confidence
- A proficiency in material at every level
- Performance to each student's full potential
- A sense of accomplishment

GETTING STARTED IS EASY. Just call us at 800.ABC.MATH or visit kumon.com to request our free brochure and find a Kumon Center near you. We'll direct you to an Instructor who will be happy to speak with you about how Kumon can address your child's particular needs and arrange a free placement test. There are more than 1,700 Kumon Centers in the U.S. and Canada, and students may enroll at any time throughout the year, even summer. Contact us today.

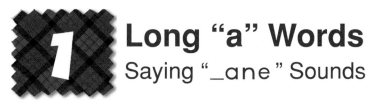

Long "a" Words
Saying "_ane" Sounds

Name

Date

To parents
Have your child write his or her name in the box above. By repeating the long "a" sound out loud, your child will gradually gain awareness of the connection between the letters and the sounds they represent.

■ Match the pictures and words by drawing a line
  from the dot (●) to the star (★). Then say the word aloud.

cane ●   ★ plane

mane ●   ★ cane

lane ●   ★ lane

plane ●   ★ mane

Saying "_ane" Sounds

■ Draw a line from the dot (●) to the star (★) while saying each word aloud.

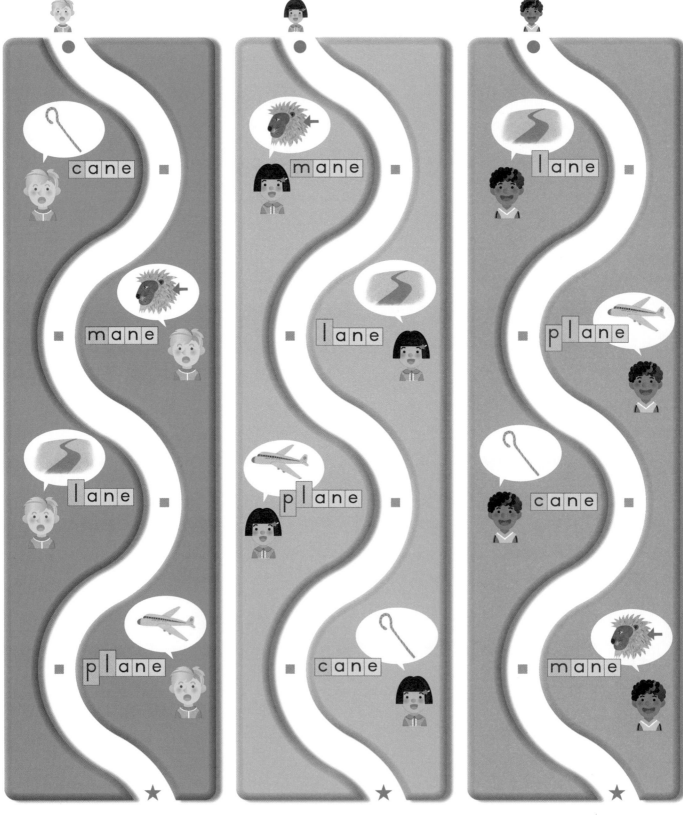

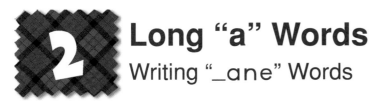

Long "a" Words
Writing "_ane" Words

Name

Date

To parents
Help your child say the words out loud. With time and practice, your child will be able to combine the letters to make the long "a" sounds.

■ Say the words aloud. Then trace the letters.

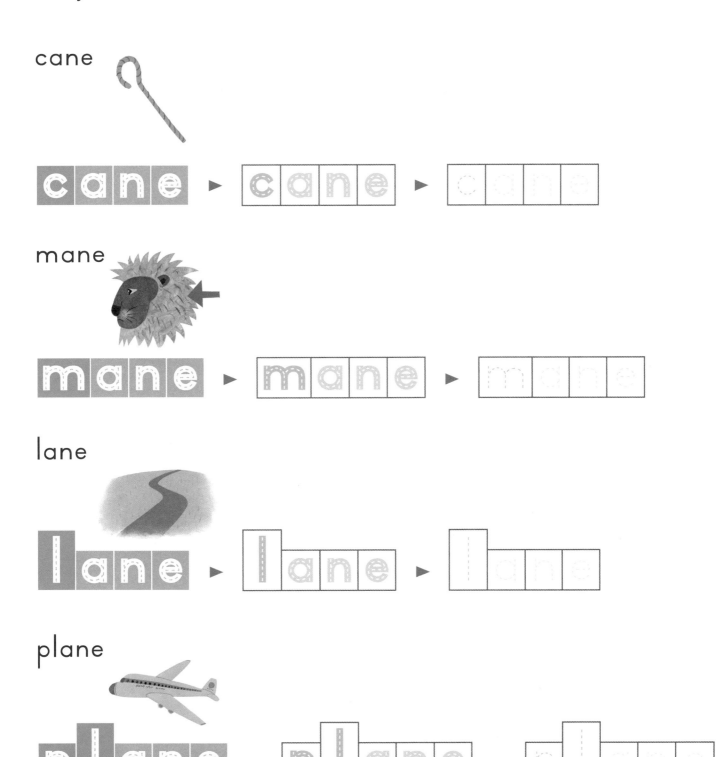

cane

mane

lane

plane

Writing "_ane" Words

■ Say the words aloud. Then trace and write the letters.

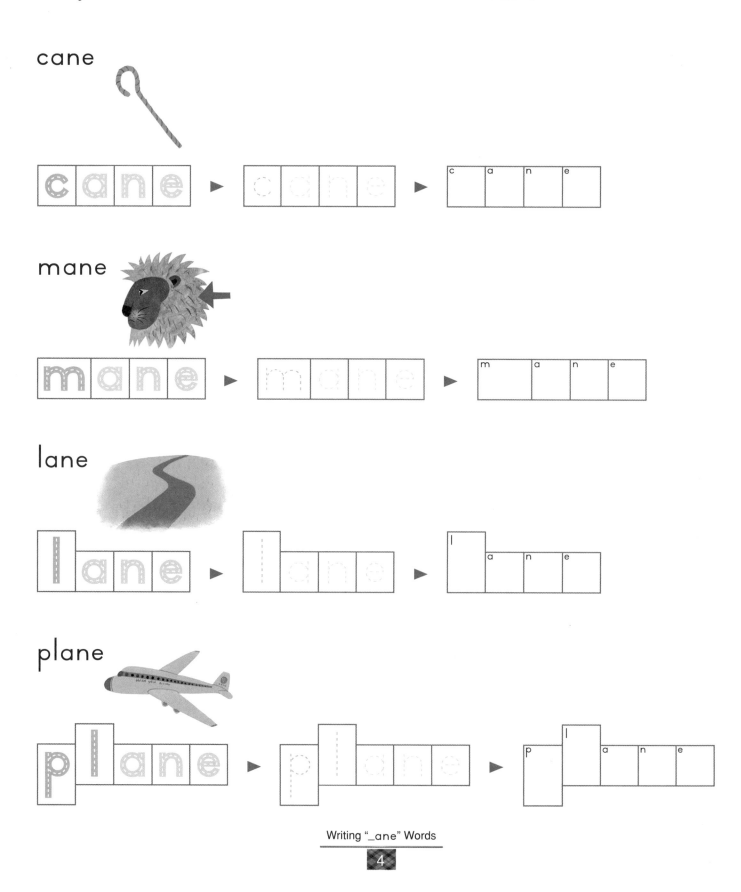

cane

mane

lane

plane

Long "a" Words
Saying "_ay" Sounds

Name

Date

■ Match the pictures and words by drawing a line
from the dot (●) to the star (★). Then say the word aloud.

hay   ●

★
play

bay   ●

★
day

day   ●

★
bay

play   ●

★
hay

Saying "_ay" Sounds

■ Draw a line from the dot (●) to the star (★) while saying each word aloud.

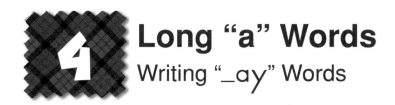

Long "a" Words
Writing "_ay" Words

Name	
Date	

■ Say the words aloud. Then trace the letters.

hay

bay

day

play

Writing "_ay" Words

■ Say the words aloud. Then trace and write the letters.

hay

bay

day

play

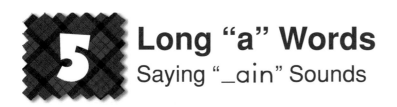

Long "a" Words
Saying "_ain" Sounds

Name

Date

■ Match the pictures and words by drawing a line
from the dot (●) to the star (★). Then say the word aloud.

rain	●
pain	●
brain	●
train	●

pain

brain

★

rain

★

train

Saying "_ain" Sounds

■ Draw a line from the dot (●) to the star (★) while saying each word aloud.

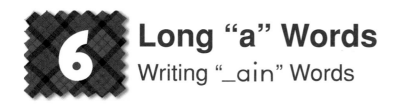

Long "a" Words
Writing "_ain" Words

■ Say the words aloud. Then trace the letters.

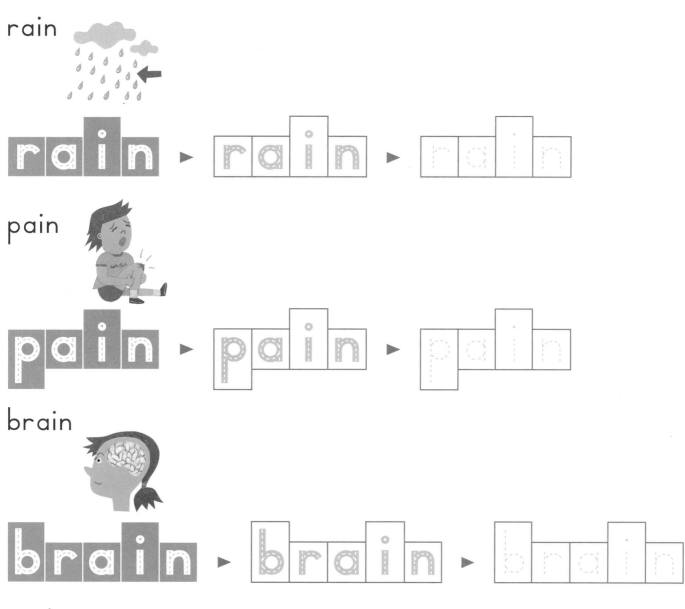

rain

rain ▶ rain ▶ rain

pain

pain ▶ pain ▶ pain

brain

brain ▶ brain ▶ brain

train

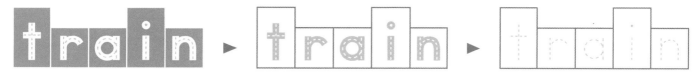

train ▶ train ▶ train

Writing "_ain" Words

■ Say the words aloud. Then trace and write the letters.

rain

pain

brain

train

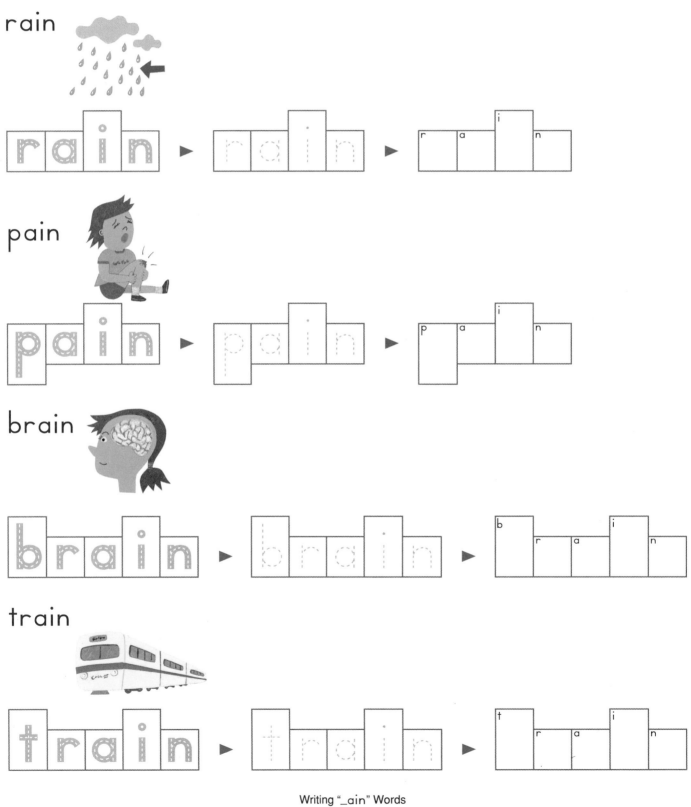

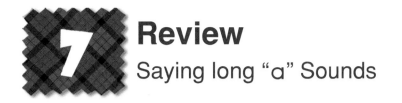

7 Review

Saying long "a" Sounds

Name

Date

■ Draw a line from 👧 to 👧 while saying "_ane" aloud.
　Draw a line from 👦 to 👦 while saying "_ay" aloud.
　Draw a line from 👧 to 👧 while saying "_ain" aloud.

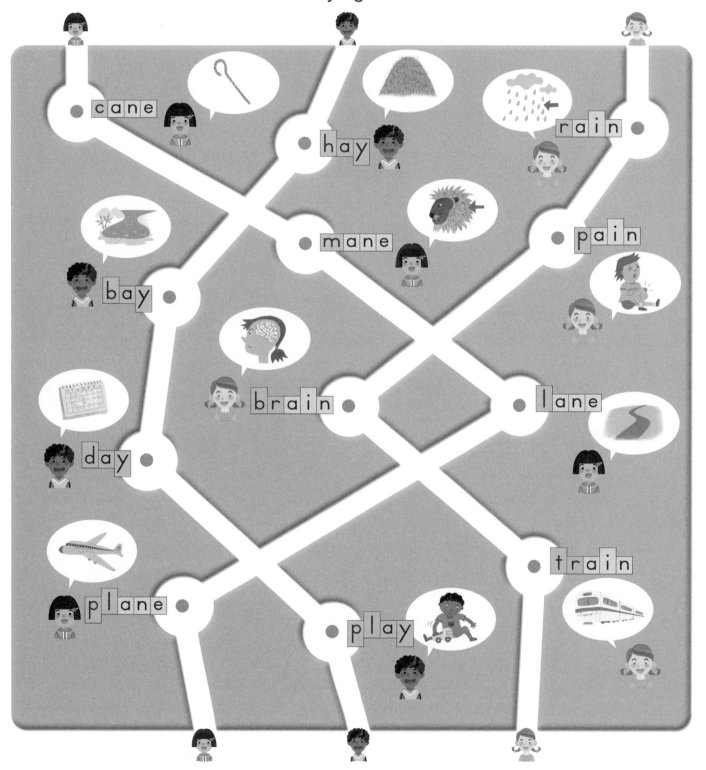

Writing "_ane," "_ay" and "_ain" Words

■ Say the words aloud. Then write the letters.

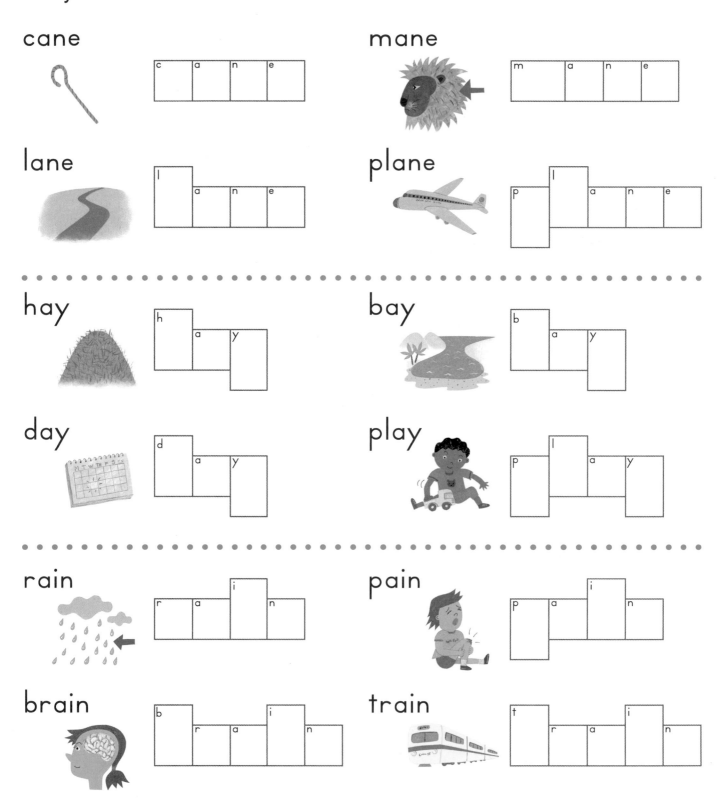

cane

mane

lane

plane

hay

bay

day

play

rain

pain

brain

train

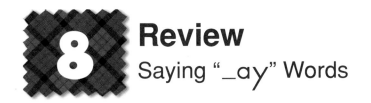

8 Review
Saying "_ay" Words

Name

Date

To parents
Once your child reaches "play," help him or her find "hay"
in order to begin the sequence again. Make sure your child
draws only vertical or horizontal lines to connect the words.

■ Draw a line from the arrow (→) to the star (★),
connecting ▲ to ▲ to ▦ to 👦 while you say the words.

hay   bay   day   play

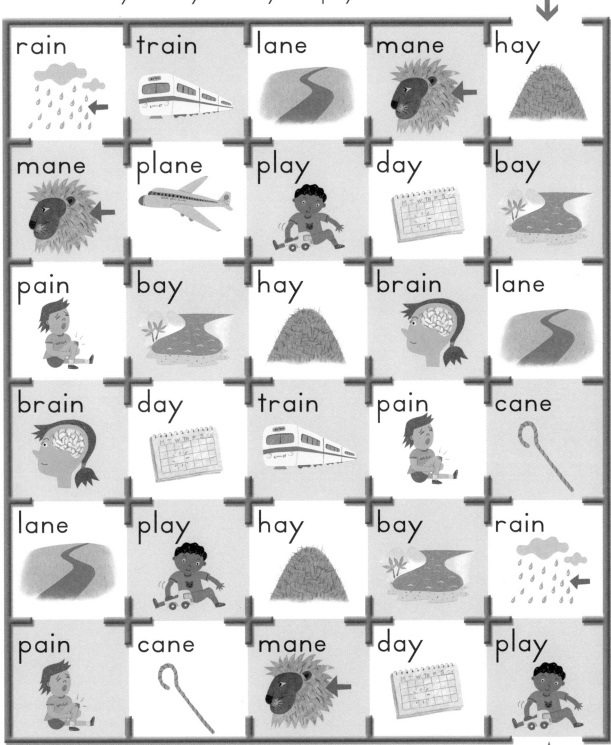

Writing "_ane," "_ay" and "_ain" Words

■ Say the words aloud. Then write the letters.

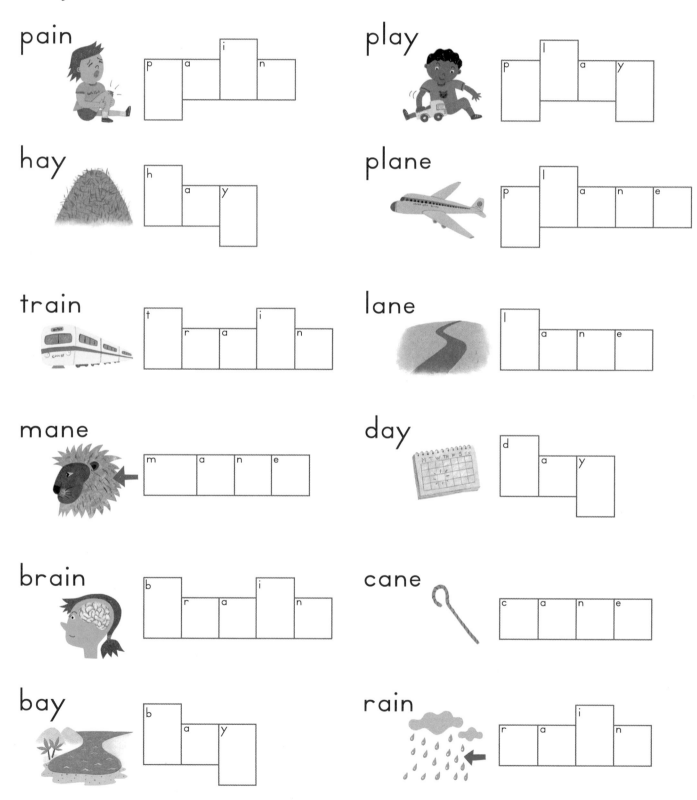

pain

play

hay

plane

train

lane

mane

day

brain

cane

bay

rain

9 Long "e" Words
Saying "_ee" Sounds

To parents
By repeating the long "e" sound out loud, your child will gradually gain awareness of the connection between the letters and the sounds they represent.

Name

Date

■ Match the pictures and words by drawing a line from the dot (●) to the star (★). Then say the word aloud.

bee	●

★
tree

see	●

★
knee

tree	●

★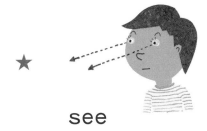
see

knee	●

★
bee

Saying "_ee" Sounds

■ Draw a line from the dot (●) to the star (★) while saying each word aloud.

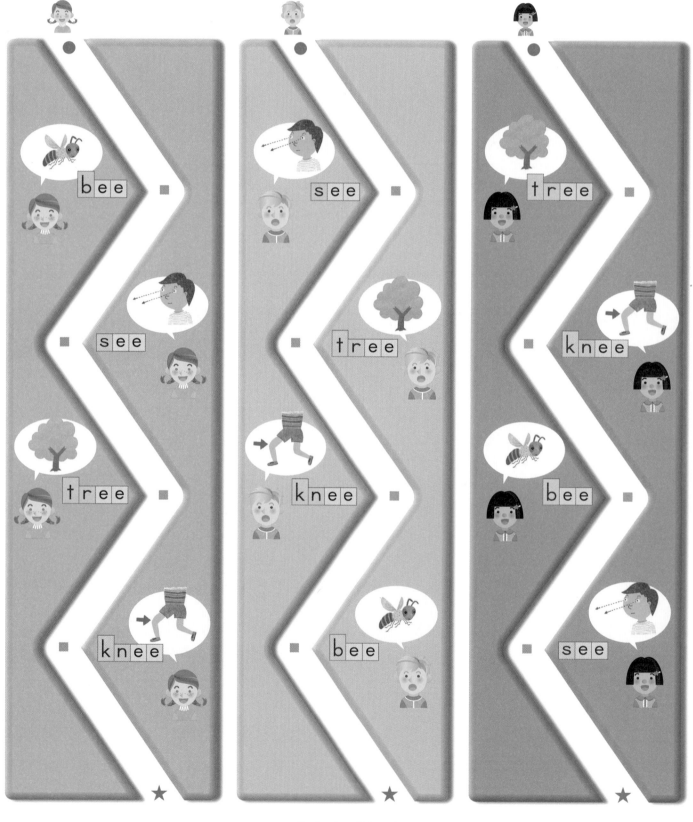

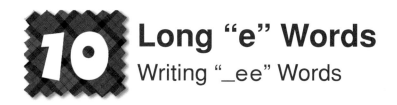

Long "e" Words
Writing "_ee" Words

Name

Date

To parents
With time and practice, your child will be able to blend the letters in order to make the long "e" sound.

■ Say the words aloud. Then trace the letters.

bee

 ▶ 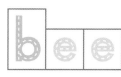 ▶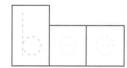

see

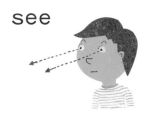

 ▶  ▶

tree

 ▶  ▶

knee

 ▶  ▶

Writing "_ee" Words

■ Say the words aloud. Then trace and write the letters.

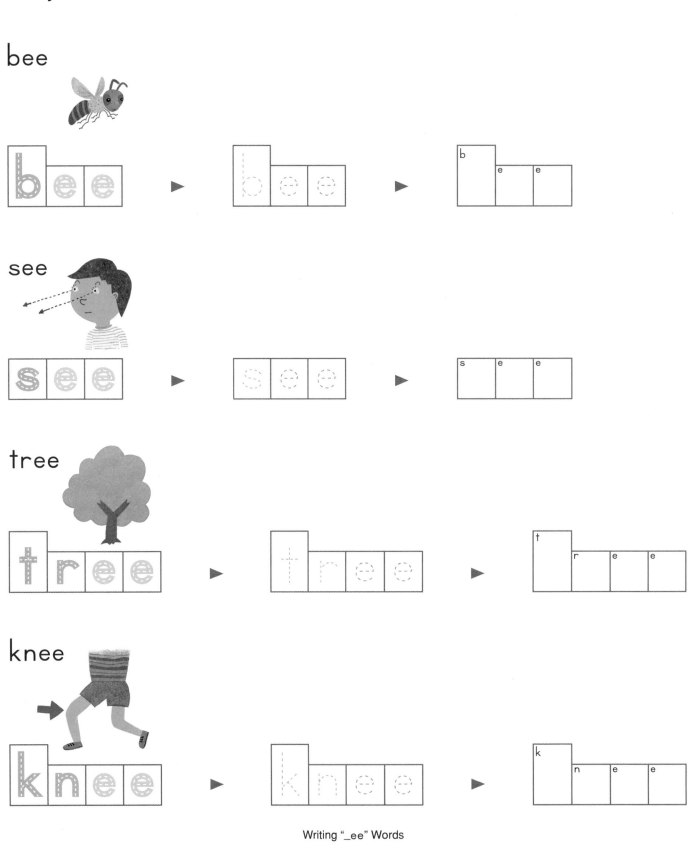

bee

see

tree

knee

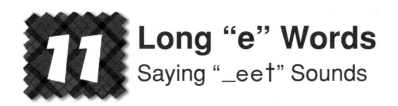

Long "e" Words
Saying "_eet" Sounds

■ Match the pictures and words by drawing a line
from the dot (●) to the star (★). Then say the word aloud.

feet	●	★	 sheet
meet	●	★	 meet
sheet	●	★	street
street	●	★	 feet

Saying "_eet" Sounds

■ Draw a line from the dot (●) to the star (★) while saying each word aloud.

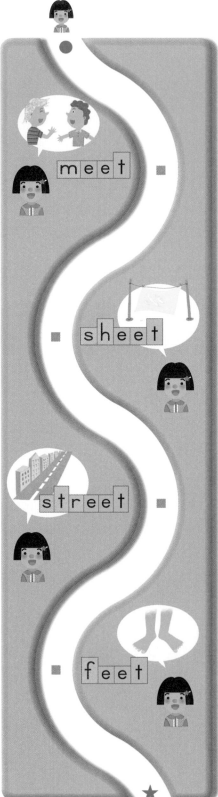

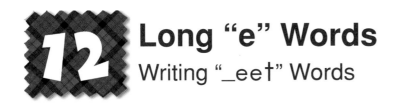

Long "e" Words
Writing "_eet" Words

Name

Date

■ Say the words aloud. Then trace the letters.

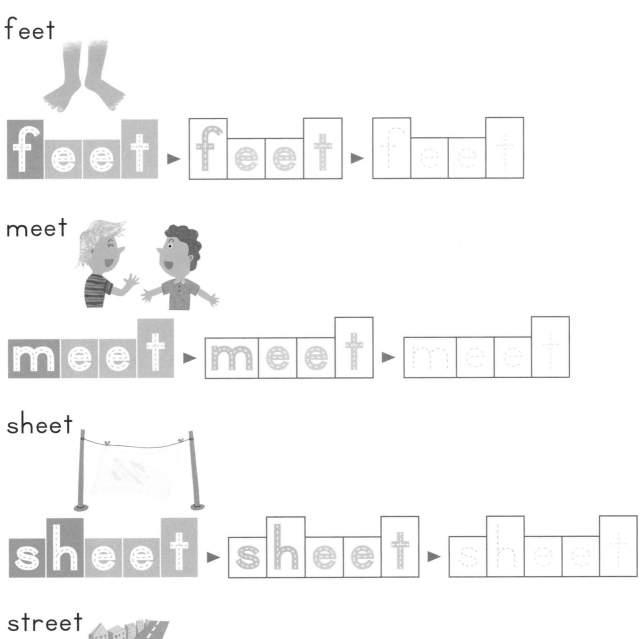

feet

meet

sheet

street

Writing "_eet" Words

■ Say the words aloud. Then trace and write the letters.

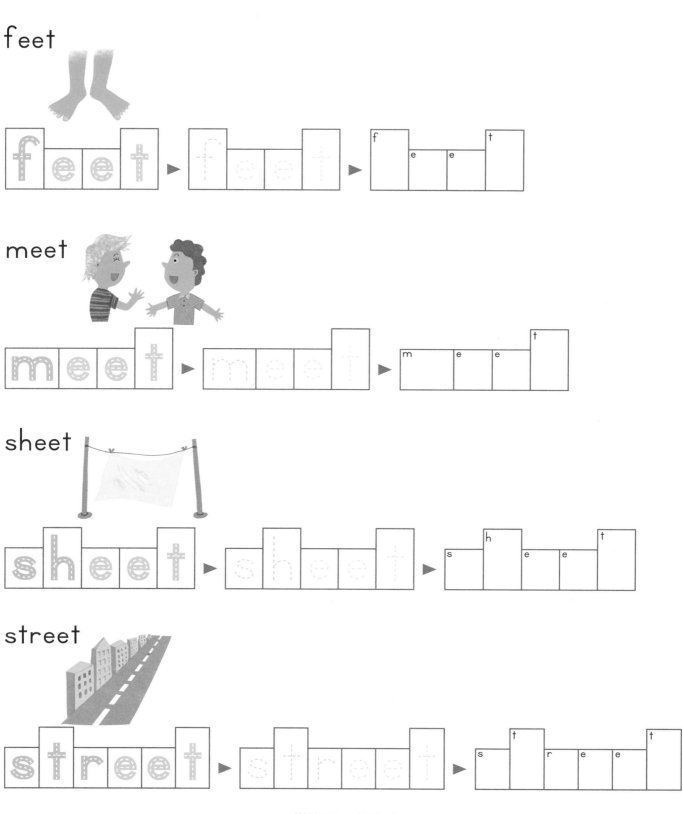

feet

meet

sheet

street

13 Long "e" Words
Saying "_eat" Sounds

Name

Date

■ Match the pictures and words by drawing a line
  from the dot (●) to the star (★). Then say the word aloud.

| meat | ● | ★ |  meat |

| seat | ● | ★ |  heat |

| heat | ● | ★ |  neat |

| neat | ● | ★ |  seat |

Saying "_eat" Sounds

■ Draw a line from the dot (●) to the star (★) while saying each word aloud.

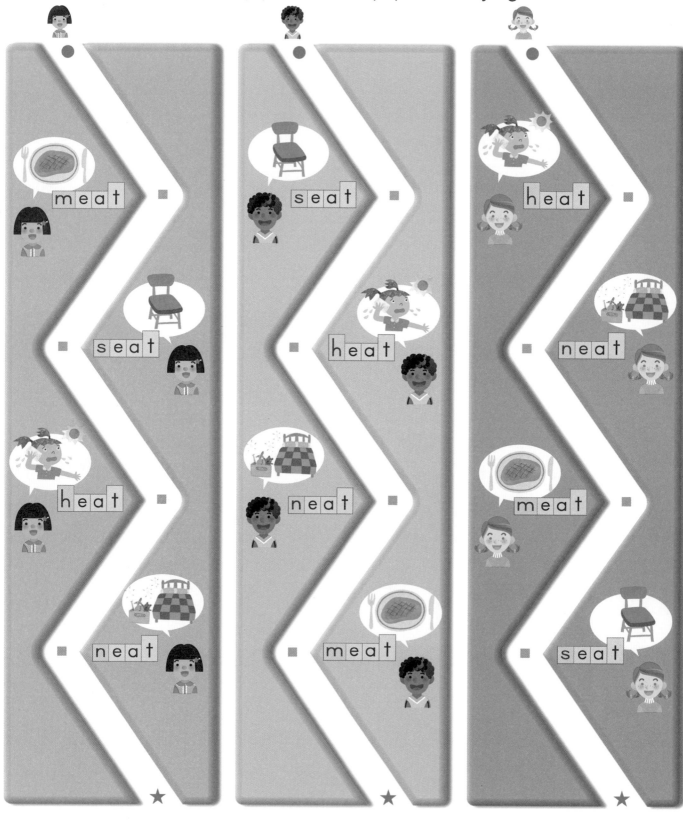

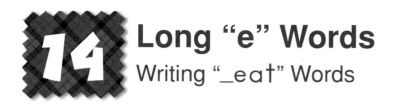

14 Long "e" Words
Writing "_eat" Words

Name

Date

■ Say the words aloud. Then trace the letters.

meat

 ▶  ▶

seat

 ▶  ▶

heat

 ▶  ▶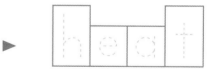

neat

 ▶  ▶

Writing "_eat" Words

■ Say the words aloud. Then trace and write the letters.

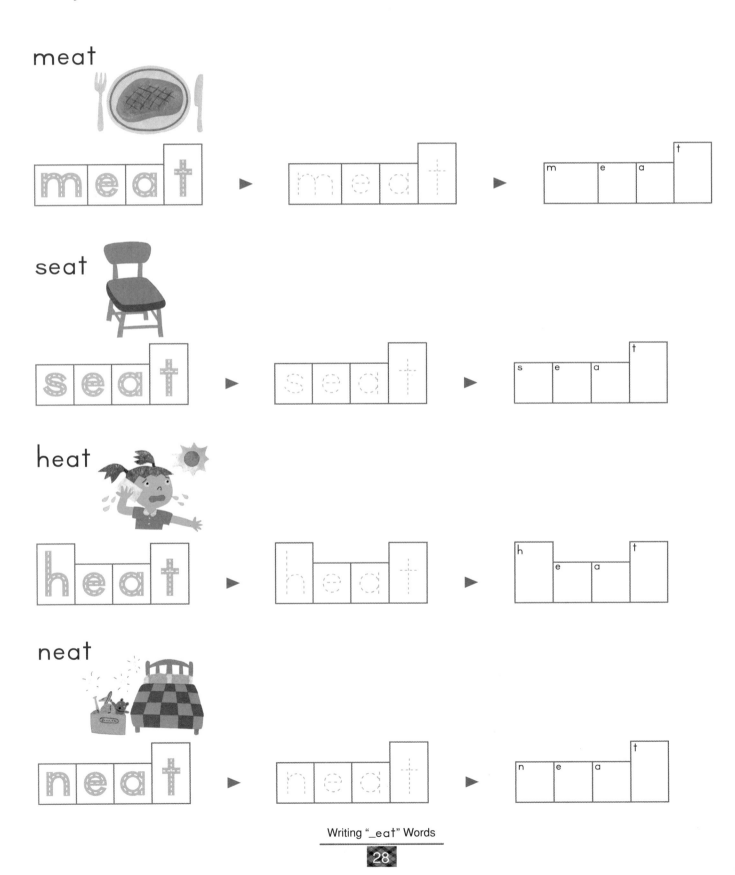

meat

seat

heat

neat

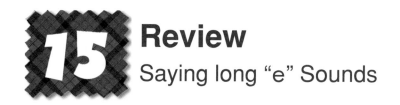

Review

Saying long "e" Sounds

■ Draw a line from 👦 to 👦 while saying each "_ee" aloud.
  Draw a line from 👧 to 👧 while saying each "_eet" aloud.
  Draw a line from 👦 to 👦 while saying each "_eat" aloud.

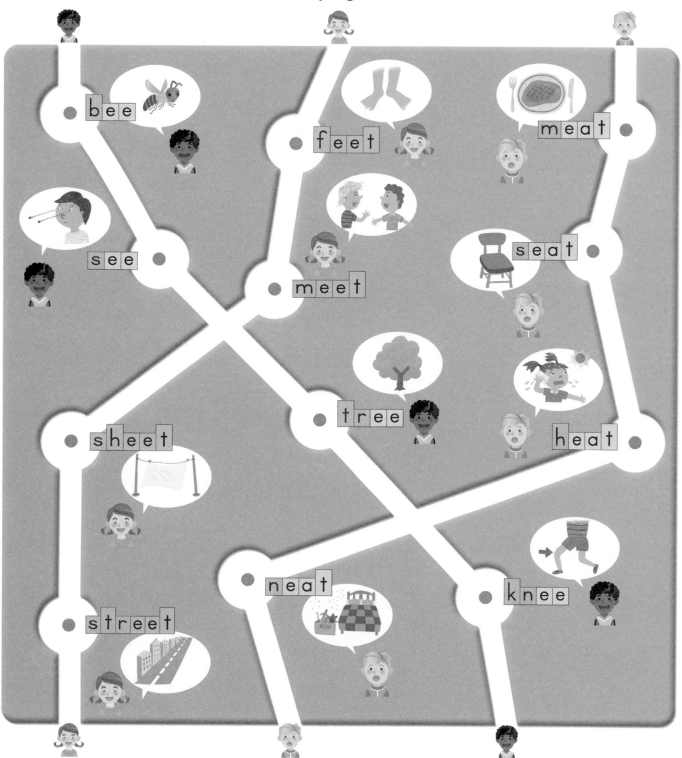

Writing "_ee," "_eet" and "_eat" Words

■ Say the words aloud. Then write the letters.

bee

b		
	e	e

see

s	e	e

tree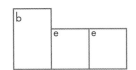

t			
	r	e	e

knee

k			
	n	e	e

feet

f			t
	e	e	

meet

			t
m	e	e	

sheet

	h		t
s		e	e

street

	t			t
s		r	e	e

meat

			t
m	e	a	

seat

			t
s	e	a	

heat

h			t
	e	a	

neat

			t
n	e	a	

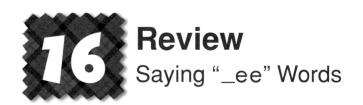

16 Review
Saying "_ee" Words

■ Draw a line from the arrow (→) to the star (★), connecting 🐝 to 👦 to 🌳 to 🏃 while you say the words.

bee   see   tree   knee

Writing "_ee," "_eet" and "_eat" Words

■ **Say the words aloud. Then write the letters.**

neat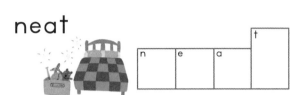

| n | e | a | t |

sheet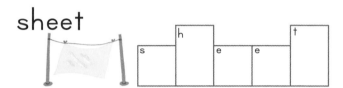

| s | h | e | e | t |

bee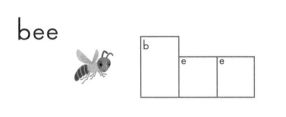

| b | e | e |

feet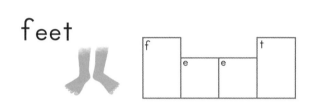

| f | e | e | t |

tree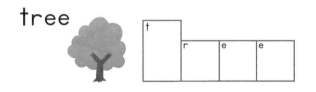

| t | r | e | e |

street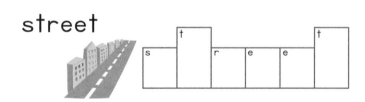

| s | t | r | e | e | t |

see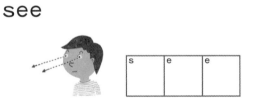

| s | e | e |

meat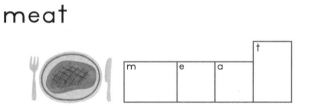

| m | e | a | t |

heat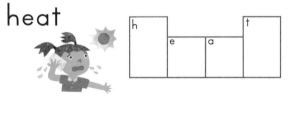

| h | e | a | t |

knee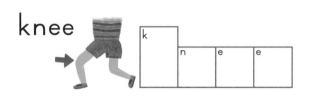

| k | n | e | e |

meet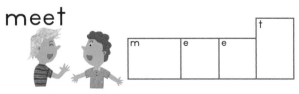

| m | e | e | t |

seat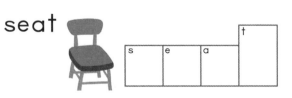

| s | e | a | t |

Long "i" Words
Saying "_ide" Sounds

Name

Date

To parents
By repeating the long "i" sound out loud, your child will gradually gain awareness of the connection between the letters and the sounds they represent.

■ Match the pictures and words by drawing a line from the dot (●) to the star (★). Then say the word aloud.

hide ●

★ slide

ride ●

★ hide

wide ●

★ wide

slide ●

★ ride

Saying "_ide" Sounds

■ Draw a line from the dot (●) to the star (★) while saying each word aloud.

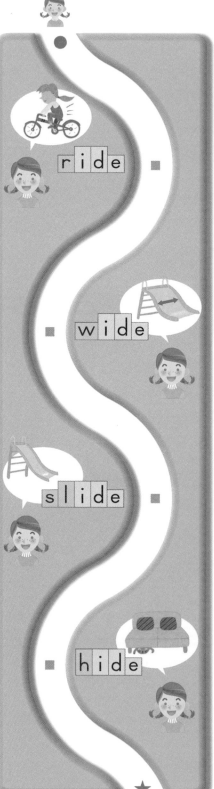
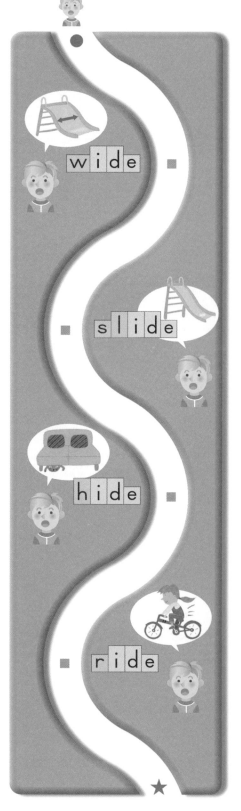

18 Long "i" Words
Writing "_ide" Words

Name

Date

To parents
With time and practice, your child will be able to blend the letters in order to make the long "i" sound.

■ Say the words aloud. Then trace the letters.

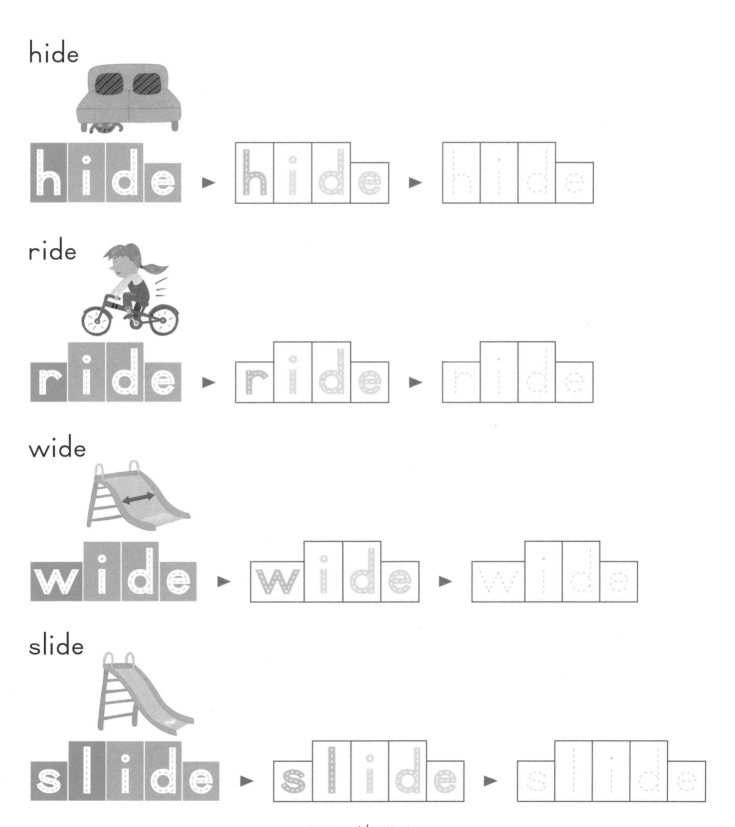

hide

ride

wide

slide

Writing "_ide" Words

■ Say the words aloud. Then trace and write the letters.

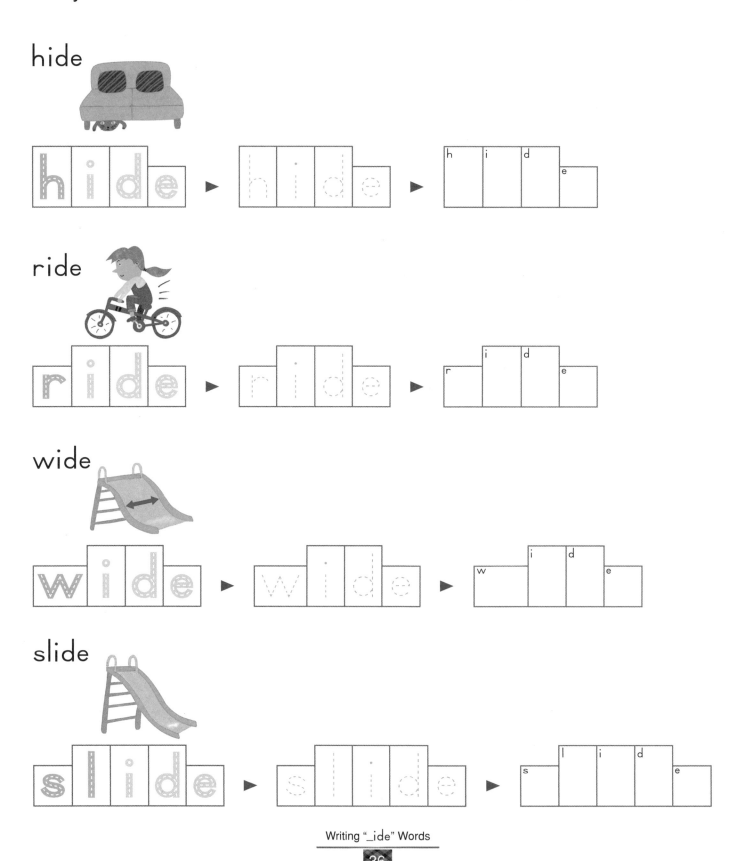

hide

ride

wide

slide

Long "i" Words
Saying "_ite" Sounds

■ Match the pictures and words by drawing a line
   from the dot (●) to the star (★). Then say the word aloud.

| bite | ● | ★ |  write |

| kite | ● | ★ | bite |

| white | ● | ★ | kite |

| write | ● | ★ | white |

Saying "_ite" Sounds

■ Draw a line from the dot (●) to the star (★) while saying each word aloud.

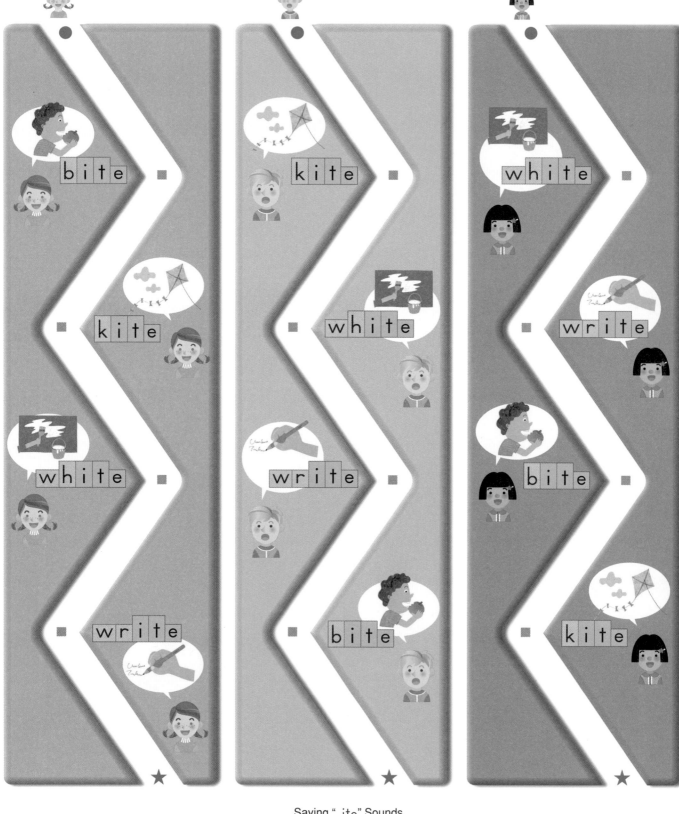

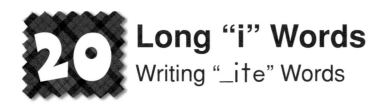

20 Long "i" Words
Writing "_ite" Words

Name

Date

■ Say the words aloud. Then trace the letters.

bite

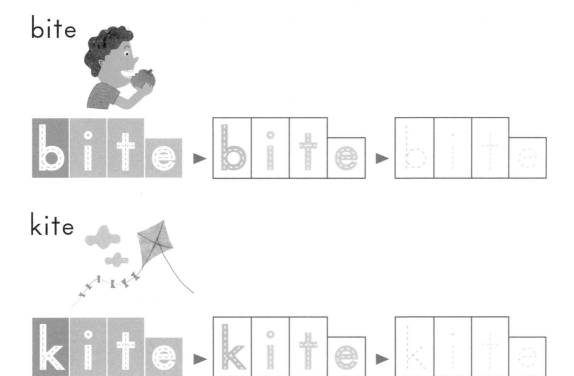

kite

white

write

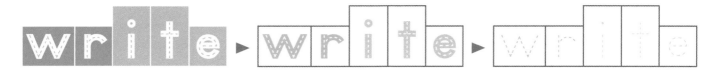

Writing "_ite" Words

■ Say the words aloud. Then trace and write the letters.

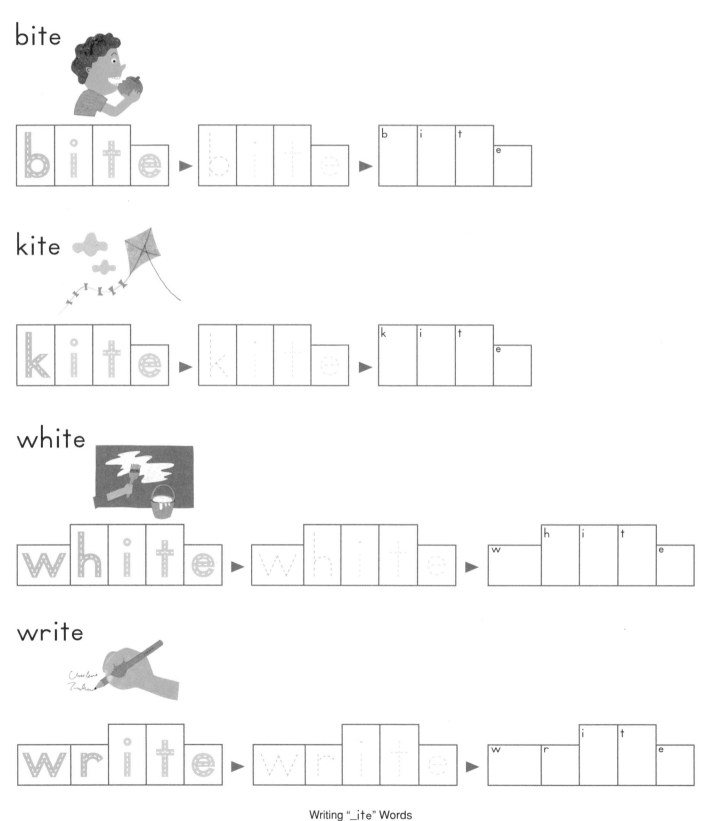

bite

kite

white

write

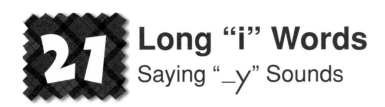

Long "i" Words
Saying "_y" Sounds

Name

Date

■ Match the pictures and words by drawing a line
from the dot (●) to the star (★). Then say the word aloud.

cry ●

★
fly

fly ●

★
fry

sky ●

★
sky

fry ●

★
cry

Saying "_y" Sounds

■ Draw a line from the dot (●) to the star (★) while saying each word aloud.

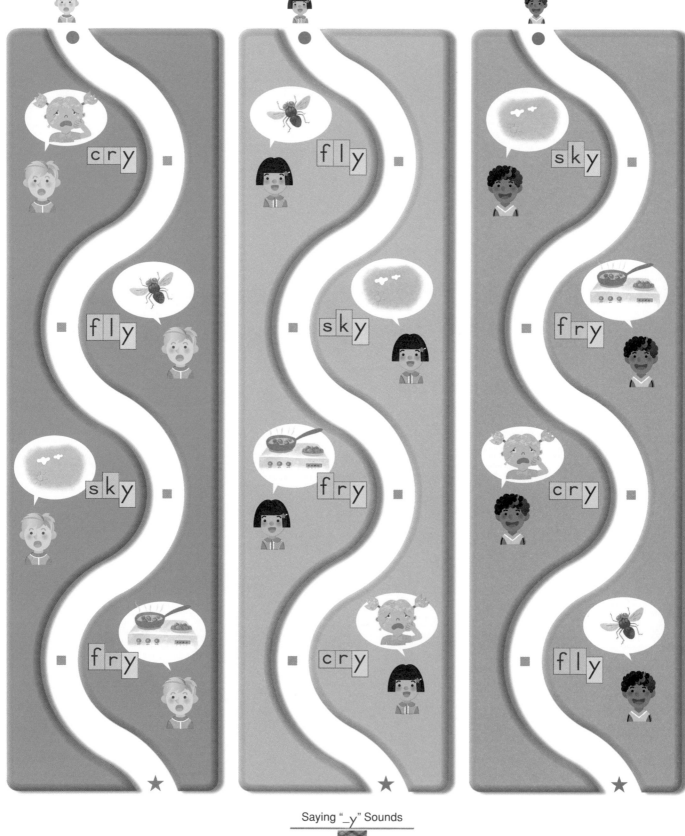

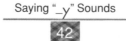

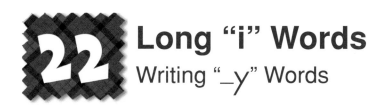

22 Long "i" Words

Writing "_y" Words

■ Say the words aloud. Then trace the letters.

cry

cry ► cry ► cry

fly

fly ► fly ► fly

sky

sky ► sky ► sky

fry

fry ► fry ► fry

Writing "_y" Words

■ Say the words aloud. Then trace and write the letters.

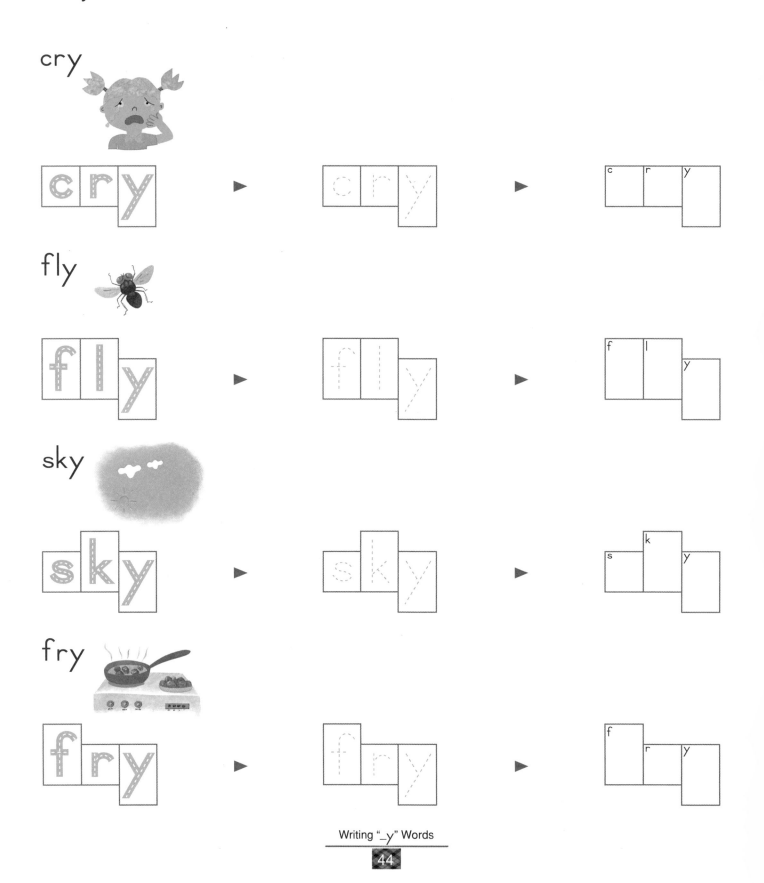

cry

fly

sky

fry

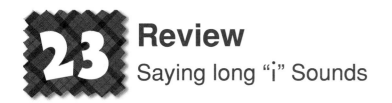

Review
Saying long "i" Sounds

■ Draw a line from 👧 to 👧 while saying each "_ide" aloud.
  Draw a line from 👦 to 👦 while saying each "_ite" aloud.
  Draw a line from 👧 to 👧 while saying each "_y" aloud.

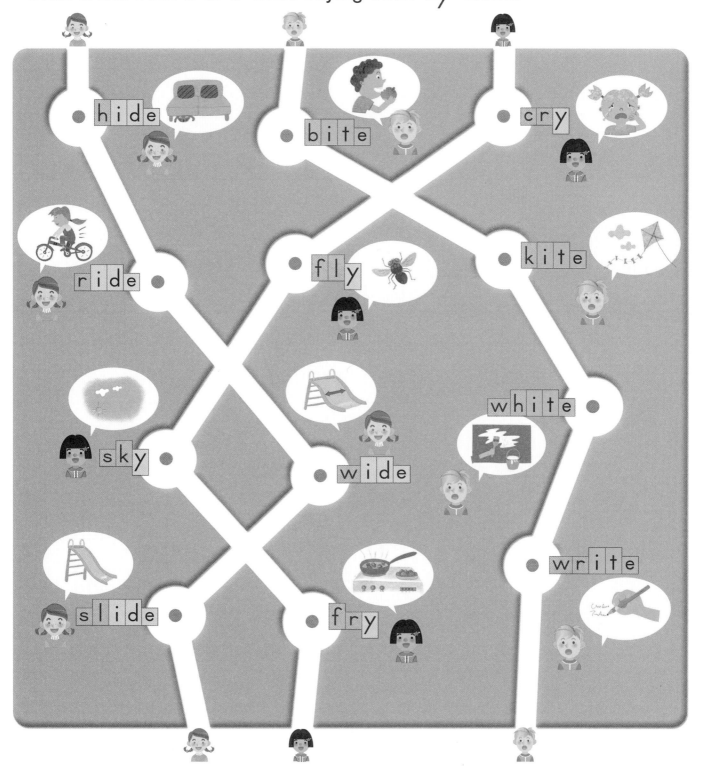

Writing "_ide," "_ite" and "_y" Words

■ Say the words aloud. Then write the letters.

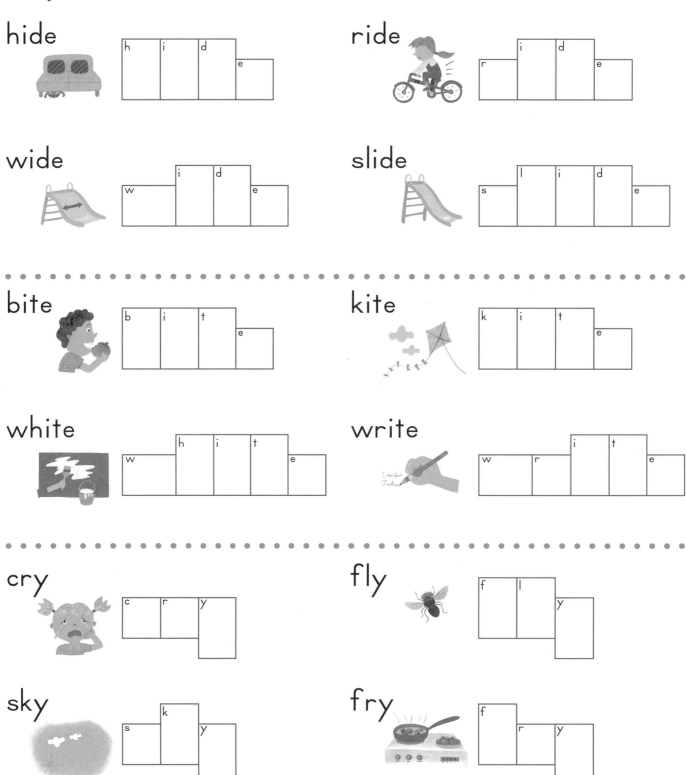

hide

| h | i | d | e |

ride

| r | i | d | e |

wide

| w | i | d | e |

slide

| s | l | i | d | e |

bite

| b | i | t | e |

kite

| k | i | t | e |

white

| w | h | i | t | e |

write

| w | r | i | t | e |

cry

| c | r | y |

fly

| f | l | y |

sky

| s | k | y |

fry

| f | r | y |

Review

Saying "_y" Words

■ Draw a line from the arrow (→) to the star (★), connecting 🧒 to 🪰 to ☁️ to 🍳 while you say the words.

cry   fly   sky   fry

write	bite	ride	wide	cry
white	hide	kite	write	fly
kite	fly	cry	fry	sky
hide	sky	bite	slide	ride
write	fry	wide	write	white
slide	cry	fly	sky	fry

Writing "_ide," "_ite" and "_y" Words

■ Say the words aloud. Then write the letters.

kite — k | i | t | e

fry — f | r | y

ride — r | i | d | e

cry — c | r | y

sky — s | k | y

write — w | r | i | t | e

bite — b | i | t | e

slide — s | l | i | d | e

wide — w | i | d | e

white — w | h | i | t | e

hide — h | i | d | e

fly — f | l | y

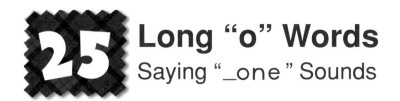

25 Long "o" Words
Saying "_one" Sounds

Name

Date

To parents
By repeating the long "o" sound out loud, your child will gradually gain awareness of the connection between the letters and the sounds they represent.

■ Match the pictures and words by drawing a line from the dot (●) to the star (★). Then say the word aloud.

bone ●	★  cone
cone ●	★  bone
phone ●	★  stone
stone ●	★  phone

Saying "_one" Sounds

■ Draw a line from the dot (●) to the star (★) while saying each word aloud.

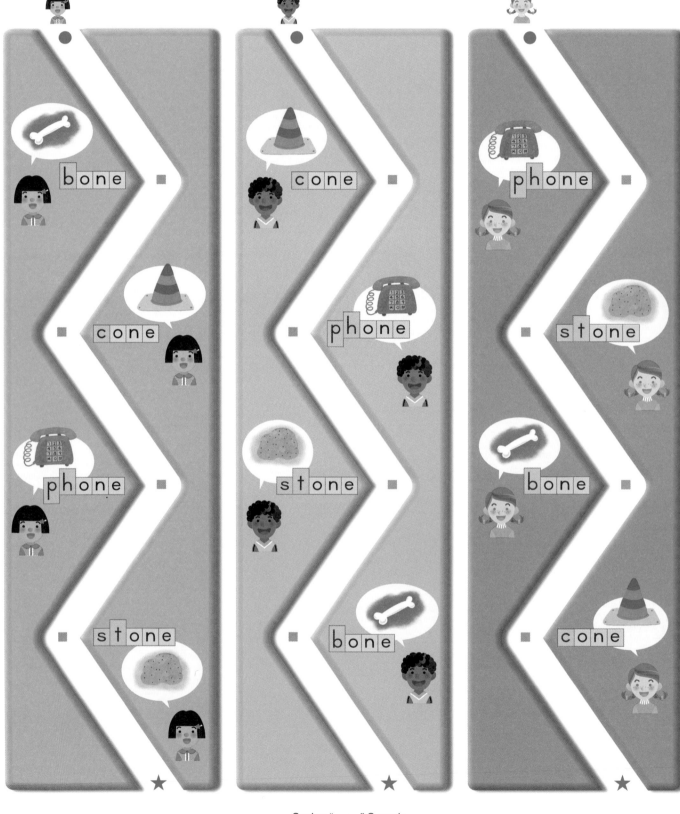

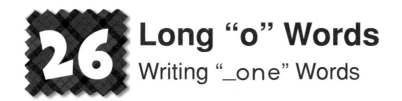

Long "o" Words

Writing "_one" Words

Name

Date

To parents
With time and practice, your child will be able to blend
the letters in order to make the long "o" sound.

■ Say the words aloud. Then trace the letters.

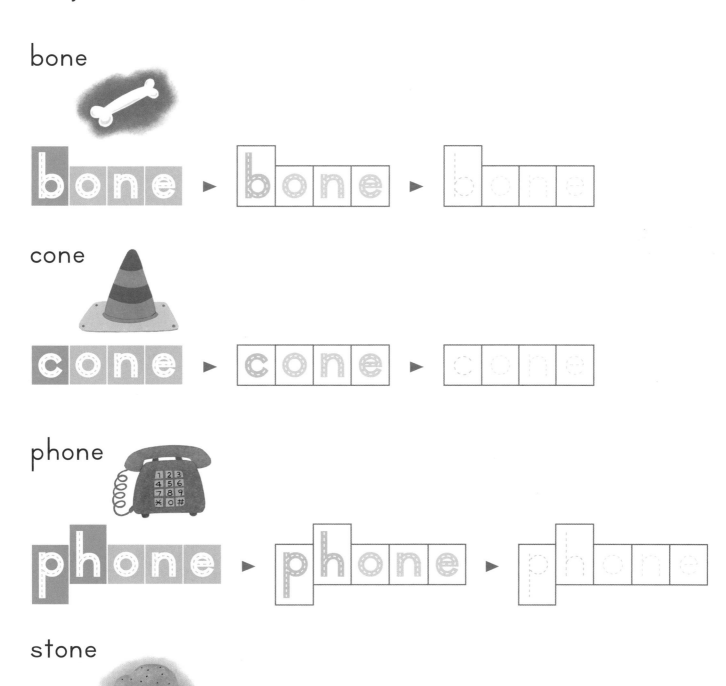

bone

cone

phone

stone

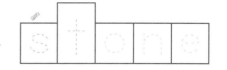

Writing "_one" Words

■ Say the words aloud. Then trace and write the letters.

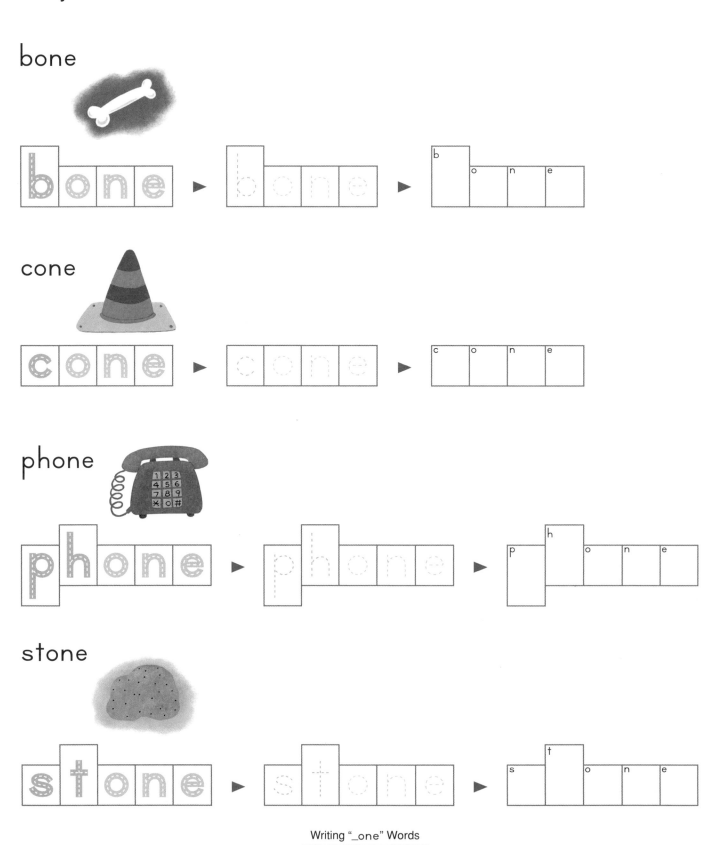

bone

cone

phone

stone

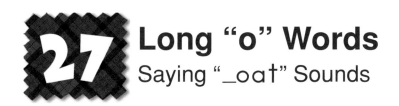

Long "o" Words
Saying "_oat" Sounds

Name

Date

■ Match the pictures and words by drawing a line
from the dot (●) to the star (★). Then say the word aloud.

boat •

★

float

coat •

★

goat

goat •

★

coat

float •

★

boat

Saying "_oat" Sounds

■ Draw a line from the dot (●) to the star (★) while saying each word aloud.

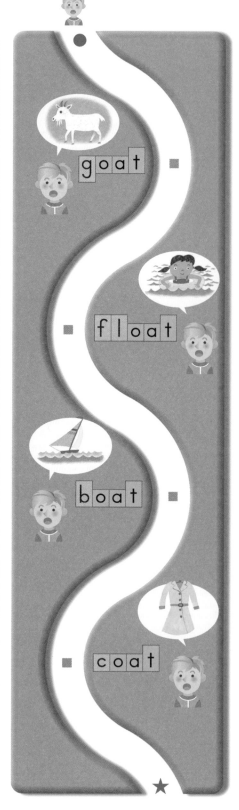

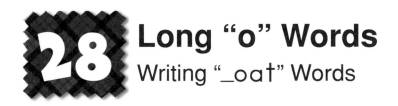

Long "o" Words
Writing "_oat" Words

Name

Date

■ Say the words aloud. Then trace the letters.

boat

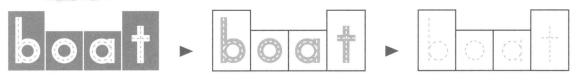

coat

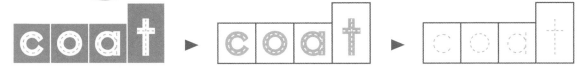

goat

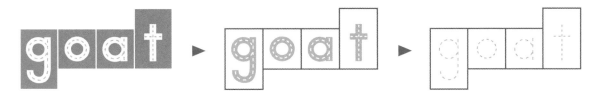

float

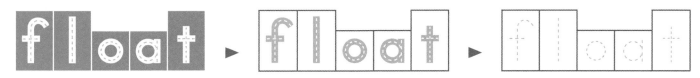

Writing "_oat" Words

■ Say the words aloud. Then trace and write the letters.

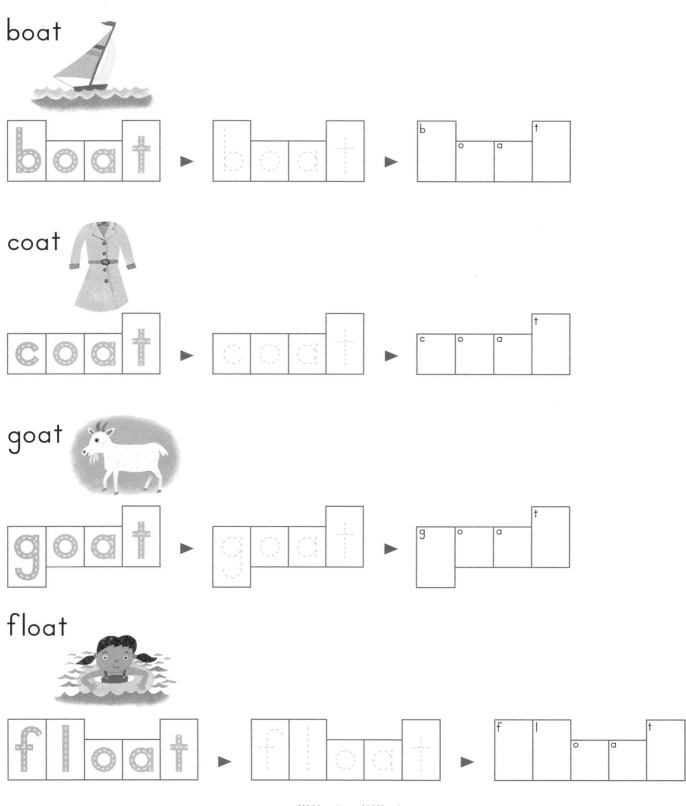

boat

coat

goat

float

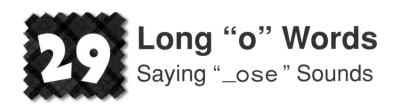

Long "o" Words
Saying "_ose" Sounds

Name

Date

■ Match the pictures and words by drawing a line
   from the dot (●) to the star (★). Then say the word aloud.

hose	●	★	 close
nose	●	★	 hose
rose	●	★	 rose
close	●	★	 nose

Saying "_ose" Sounds

■ Draw a line from the dot (●) to the star (★) while saying each word aloud.

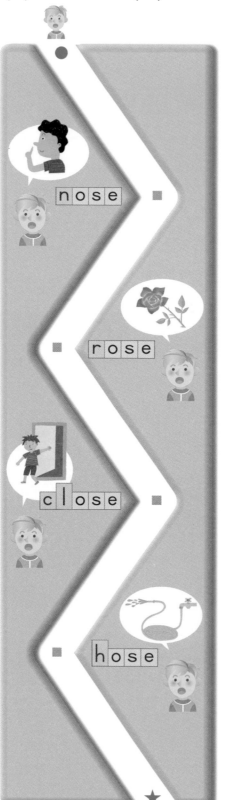
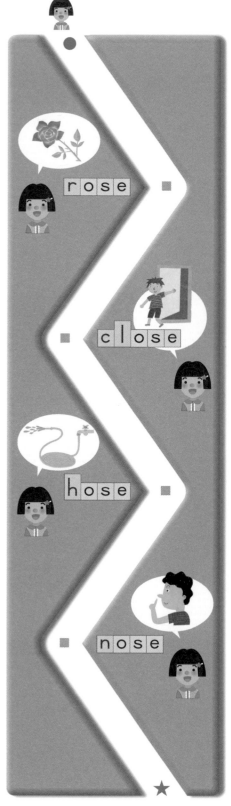

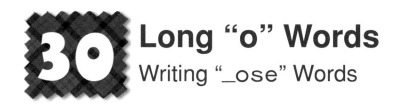

30 Long "o" Words
Writing "_ose" Words

Name

Date

■ Say the words aloud. Then trace the letters.

hose

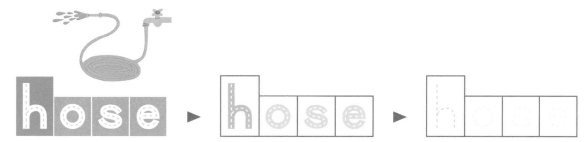

nose

rose

close

 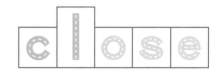 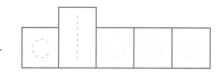

Writing "_ose" Words

■ Say the words aloud. Then trace and write the letters.

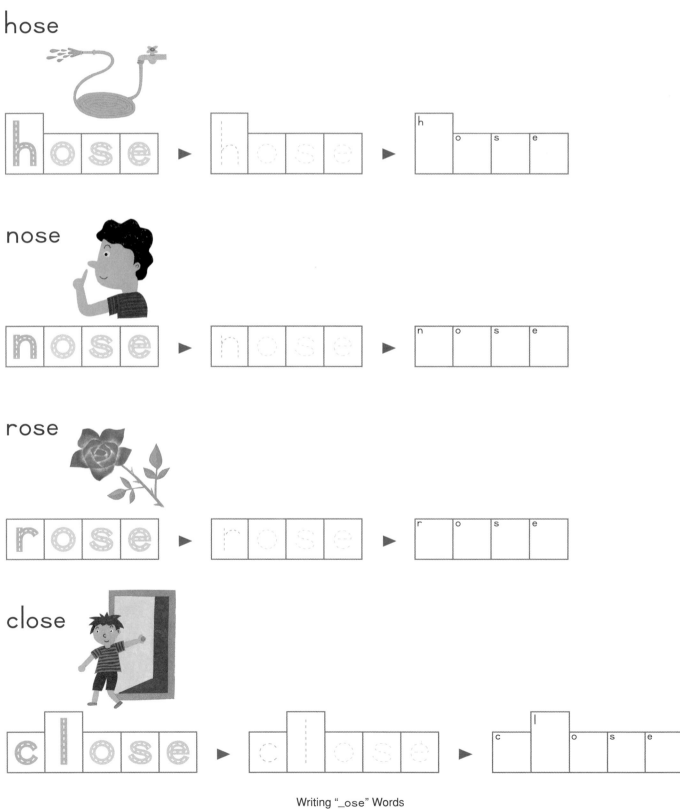

hose

nose

rose

close

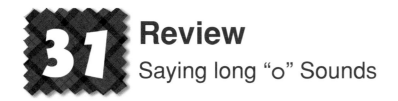

Review

Saying long "o" Sounds

Name

Date

■ Draw a line from 👦 to 👦 while saying each "_one" aloud.
  Draw a line from 👧 to 👧 while saying each "_oat" aloud.
  Draw a line from 👦 to 👦 while saying each "_ose" aloud.

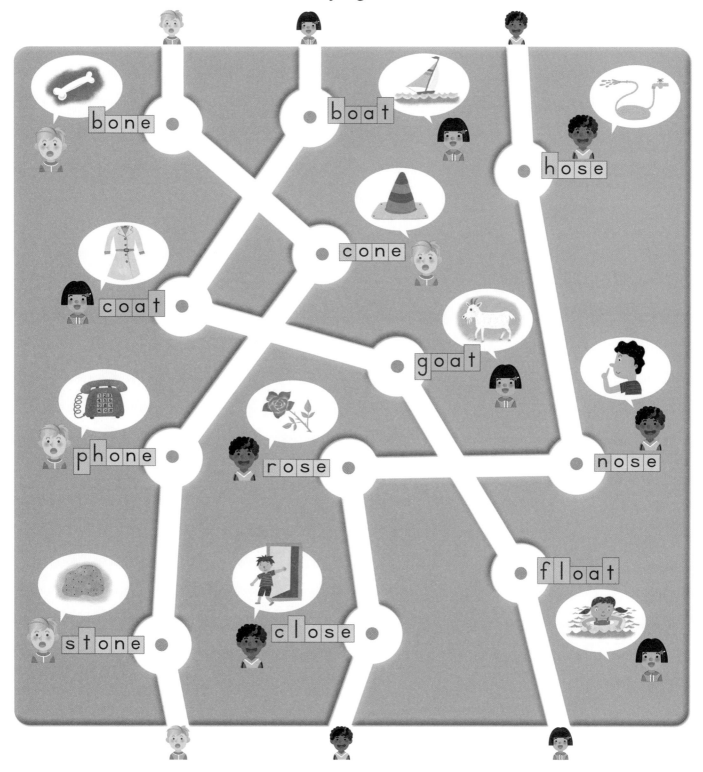

Writing "_one," "_oat" and "_ose" Words

■ Say the words aloud. Then write the letters.

bone

| b | | | |
| | o | n | e |

cone

| c | o | n | e |

phone

| | h | | | |
| p | | o | n | e |

stone

| | t | | | |
| s | | o | n | e |

boat

| b | | | t |
| | o | a | |

coat

| c | o | a | t |
| | | | |

goat

| g | | | t |
| | o | a | |

float

| f | l | | t |
| | | o | a | |

hose

| h | | | |
| | o | s | e |

nose

| n | o | s | e |

rose

| r | o | s | e |

close

| | l | | |
| c | | o | s | e |

Name

Date

■ Draw a line from the arrow (→) to the star (★),
connecting  to ⚠ to ☎ to ● while you say the words.

bone   cone   phone   stone

↓

goat	stone	phone	cone	bone
cone	bone	rose	hose	coat
phone	nose	boat	rose	float
stone	bone	close	goat	hose
coat	cone	phone	nose	close
rose	float	stone	bone	cone

★

Writing "_one," "_oat" and "_ose" Words

■ Say the words aloud. Then write the letters.

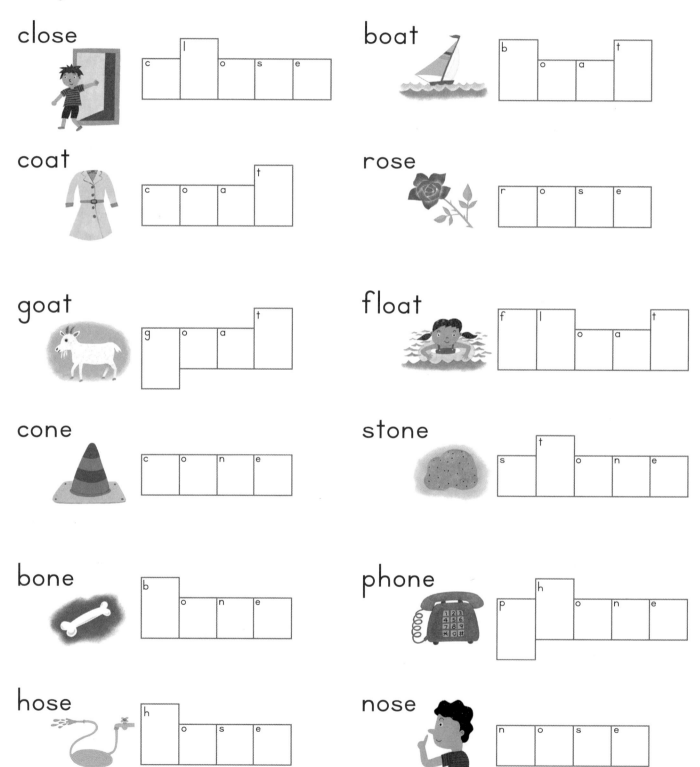

close

boat

coat

rose

goat

float

cone

stone

bone

phone

hose

nose

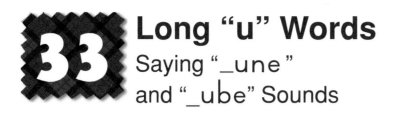

Long "u" Words

Saying "_une"
and "_ube" Sounds

Name

Date

To parents
By repeating the long "u" sound out loud, your child will
gradually gain awareness of the connection between the
letters and the sounds they represent.

■ Match the pictures and words by drawing a line
  from the dot (●) to the star (★). Then say the word aloud.

tune ●

★
cube

dune ●

★
tube

cube ●

★
tune

tube ●

★
dune

Saying "_une" and "_ube" Sounds

■ Draw a line from the dot (●) to the star (★) while saying each word aloud.

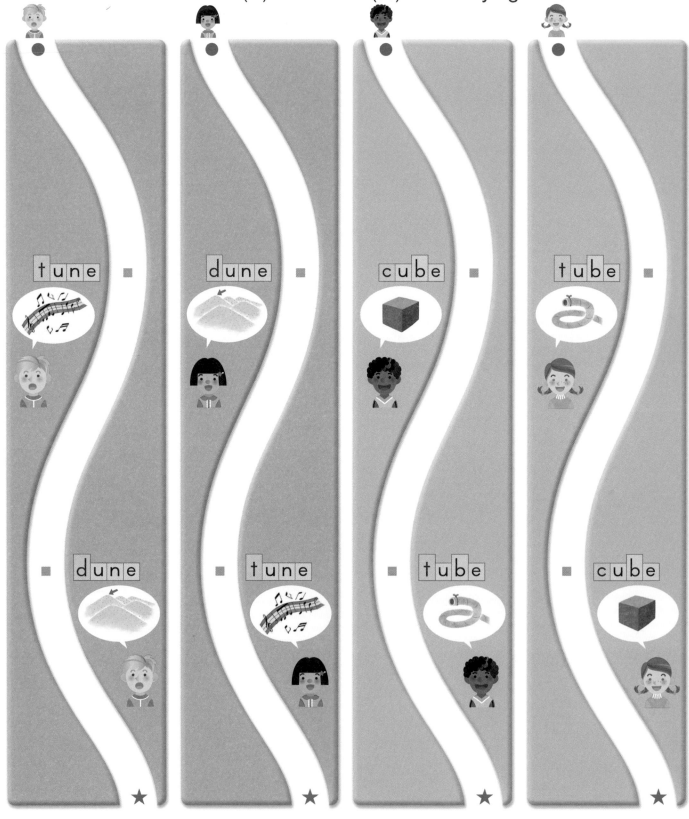

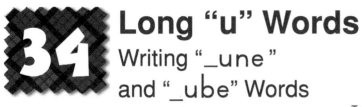

Long "u" Words

Writing "_une" and "_ube" Words

Name

Date

To parents
Help your child say the words out loud. With time and practice your child will be able to blend the letters in order to make the long "u" sound.

■ Say the words aloud. Then trace the letters.

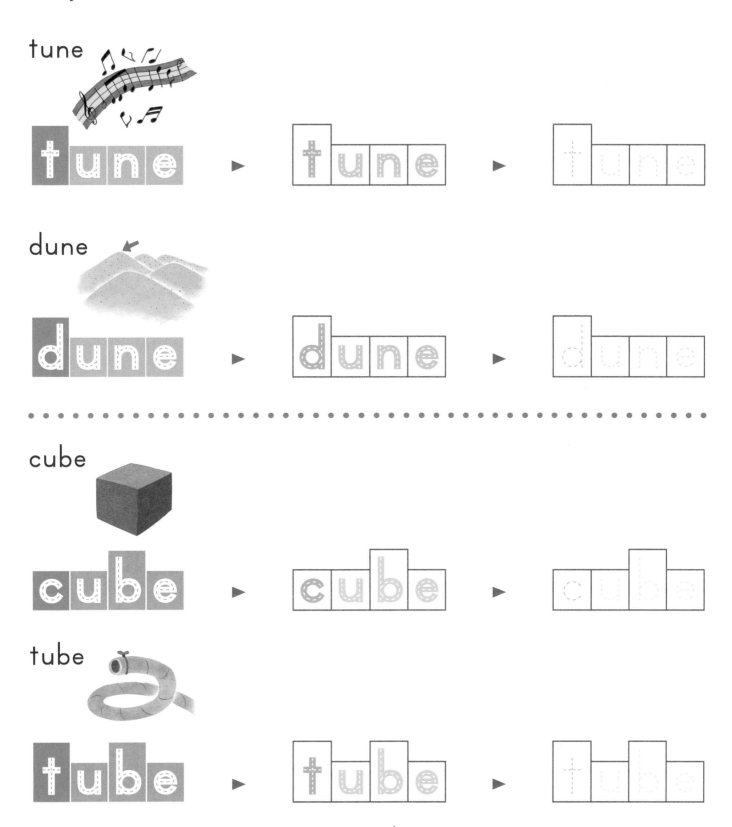

tune

dune

cube

tube

Writing "_une" and "_ube" Words

■ Say the words aloud. Then trace and write the letters.

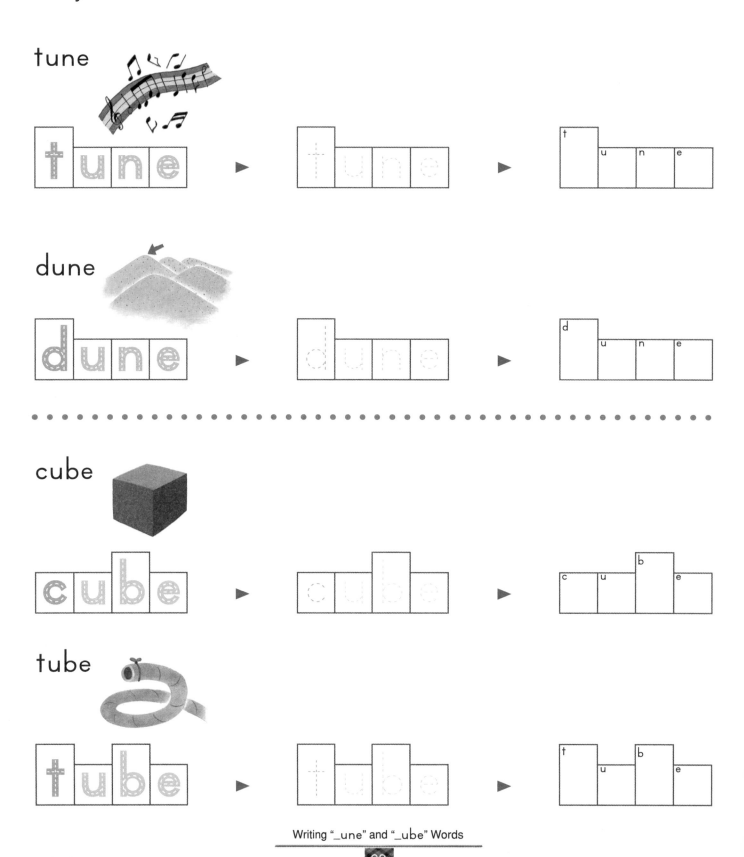

tune

dune

cube

tube

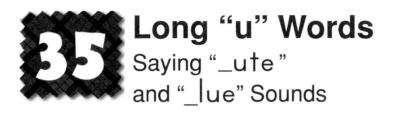

Long "u" Words
Saying "_ute"
and "_lue" Sounds

■ Match the pictures and words by drawing a line
from the dot (●) to the star (★). Then say the word aloud.

cute •

★ flute

flute •

★ glue

glue •

★ blue

blue •

★  cute

Saying "_ute" and "_lue" Sounds

■ Draw a line from the dot (●) to the star (★) while saying each word aloud.

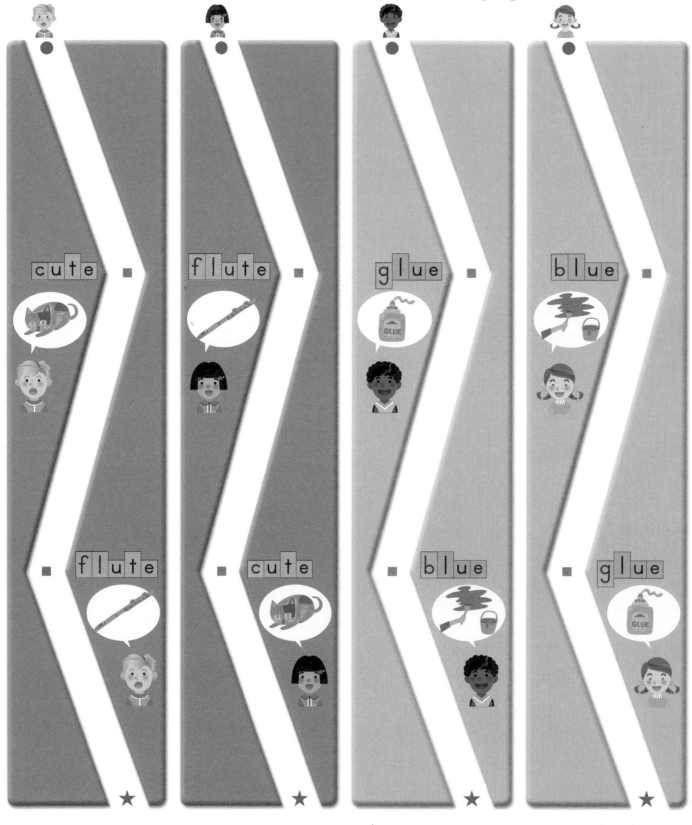

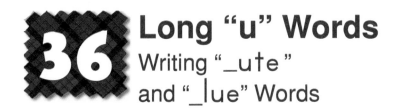

36 Long "u" Words

Writing "_ute"
and "_lue" Words

Name

Date

■ Say the words aloud. Then trace the letters.

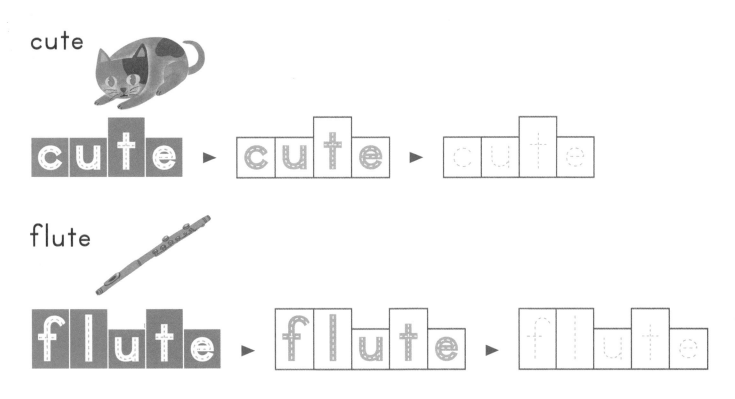

cute

cute ▶ cute ▶ cute

flute

flute ▶ flute ▶ flute

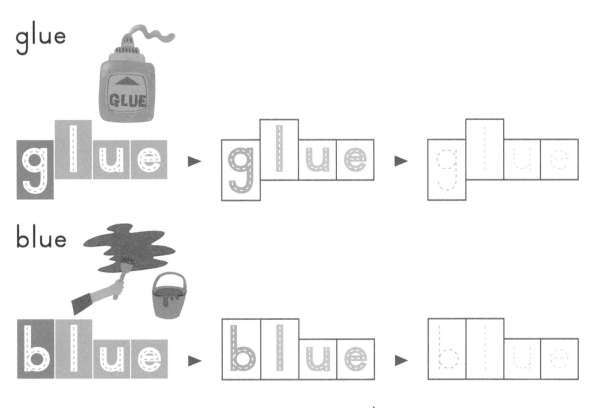

glue

glue ▶ glue ▶ glue

blue

blue ▶ blue ▶ blue

Writing "_ute" and "_lue" Words

■ Say the words aloud. Then trace and write the letters.

cute

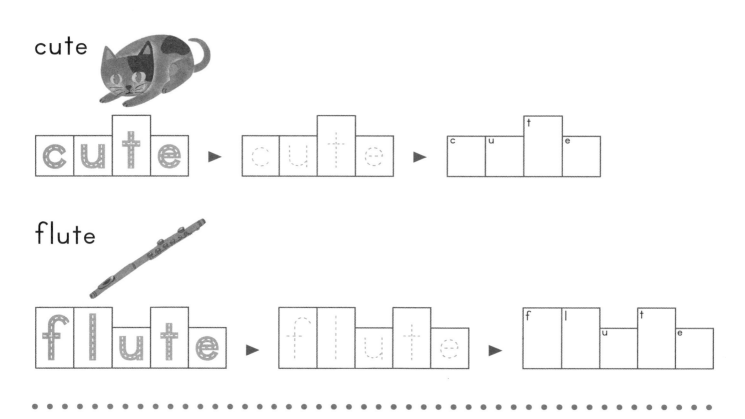

flute

· ·

glue

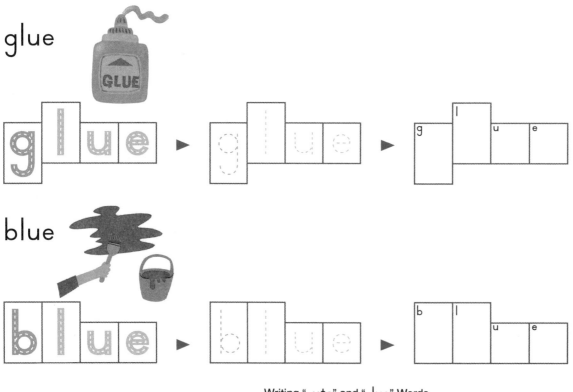

blue

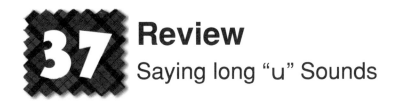

Review

Saying long "u" Sounds

■ Draw a line from 👦 to 👧 while saying each "_une" aloud.
Draw a line from 👧 to 👧 while saying each "_ube" aloud.
Draw a line from 👦 to 👦 while saying each "_ute" aloud.
Draw a line from 👧 to 👧 while saying each "_lue" aloud.

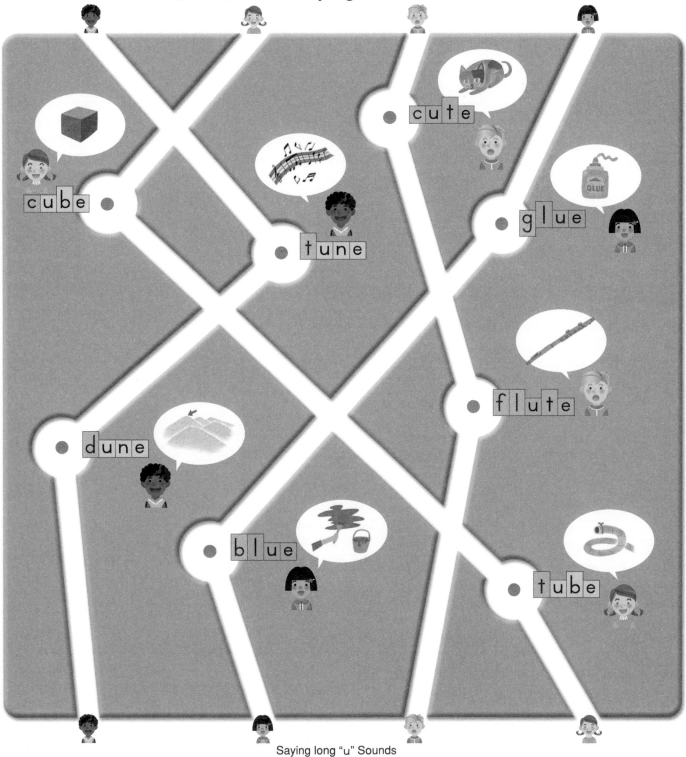

Writing "_une," "_ube," "_ute" and "_lue" Words

■ Say the words aloud. Then write the letters.

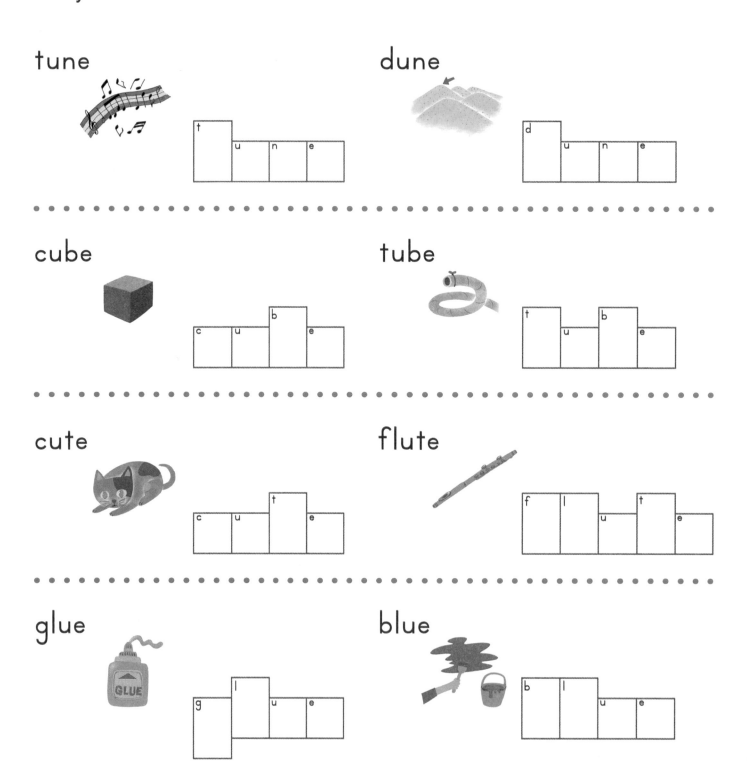

tune

dune

cube

tube

cute

flute

glue

blue

38 Review
"_ane" Stories

Name

Date

To parents
In these exercises, your child will practice using the rhyming words he or she learned throughout this book. By grouping familiar words in a new way, this exercise reinforces the words in a real-world context and emphasizes comprehension.

■ This exercise uses "_ane" words. Please use the pictures to complete the rhyming phrases below.

What is in the lane ?

①   ②   ③

① A [c][a][n][e] is in the [l][a][n][e] !

② A [m][a][n][e] is in the [l][a][n][e] !

③ A [p][l][a][n][e] is in the [l][a][n][e] !

"_ay" Stories

To parents
If your child encounters difficulty, try pointing out that each sentence has a corresponding picture associated with it. For example, if your child is struggling with sentence number one, ask them to describe picture number one.

■ This exercise uses "_ay" words. Please use the pictures to complete the rhyming phrases below.

I like to play !

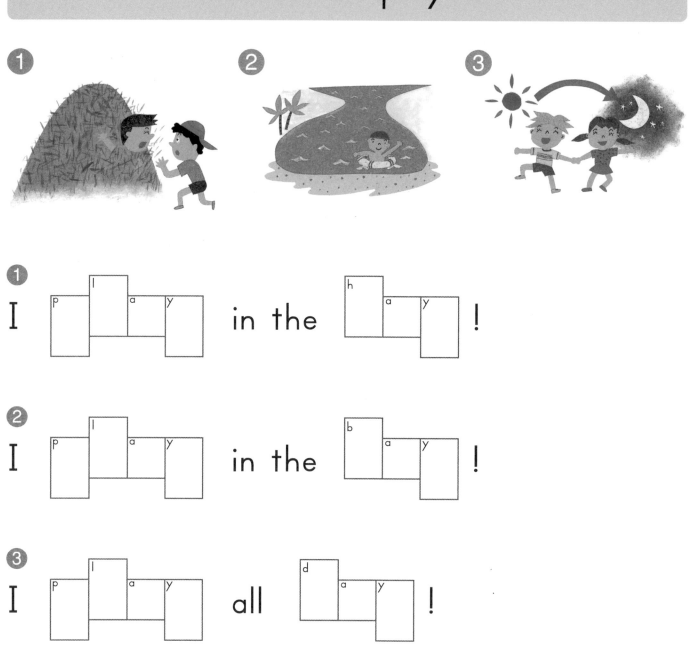

① I [p l a y] in the [h a y] !

② I [p l a y] in the [b a y] !

③ I [p l a y] all [d a y] !

Review

"_ee" Stories

To parents
If your child is confused about which picture to use with each rhyming phrase, please point out that the numbers next to the pictures correspond with the rhyming phrases below.

■ This exercise uses "_ee" words. Please use the pictures to complete the rhyming phrases below.

What do you see ?

1

I [s][e][e] a [b][e][e] !

2

I [s][e][e] a [t][r][e][e] !

3

I [s][e][e] a [k][n][e][e] !

"_oat" Stories

■ This exercise uses "_oat" words. Please use the pictures to complete the rhyming phrases below.

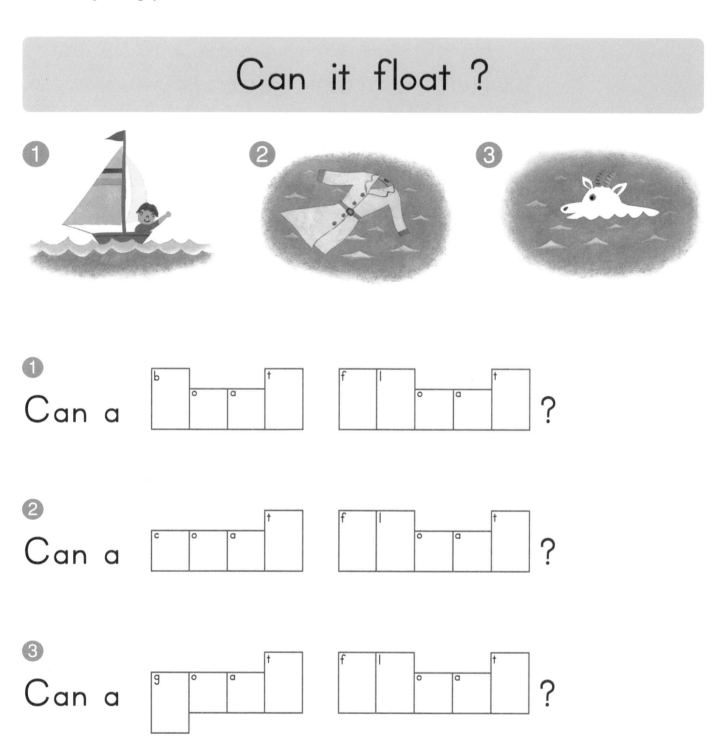

Can it float ?

1

2

3

1

Can a `b o a t` `f l o a t` ?

2

Can a `c o a t` `f l o a t` ?

3

Can a `g o a t` `f l o a t` ?

Review

"_ide" Stories

■ This exercise uses "_ide" words. Please use the pictures to complete the rhyming phrases below.

What a fun slide!

①    ②    ③

① I [r i d e] on the [s l i d e] !

② I [h i d e] by the [s l i d e] !

③ The [s l i d e] is [w i d e] !

Long "u" Stories

To parents
Your child has been using phonics to develop an understanding of new vocabulary with long vowels, which is a difficult and essential concept to learn. Please give your child lots of praise for the effort it took to achieve this goal.

■ This exercise uses long "u" words. Please use the pictures to complete the rhyming phrases below.

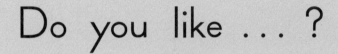

1

Do you like a [t][u][n][e] on a [d][u][n][e]?

2

Do you like [b][l][u][e] [g][l][u][e]?

3

Do you like a [c][u][t][e] [f][l][u][t][e]?

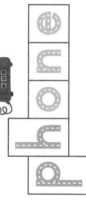

Certificate of Achievement

KUM◯N

is hereby congratulated on completing

My Book of Rhyming Words Long Vowels

Presented on _____ , 20____

_____
Parent or Guardian

 bone  cone 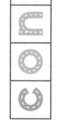 phone